Extremities

A PLAY IN TWO ACTS

by William Mastrosimone

SAMUEL FRENCH, INC.
45 WEST 25TH STREET   NEW YORK 10010
7623 SUNSET BOULEVARD   HOLLYWOOD 90046
LONDON   *TORONTO*

To Jack Bettenbender

IMPORTANT BILLING & CREDIT REQUIREMENTS

Producers of EXTREMITIES must give credit to the Author in all programs and in all instances in which the title of the Play appears for the purposes of advertising, publicizing or otherwise exploiting the Play and/or a production thereof. The name of the Author must appear on a separate line in which no other name appears, immediately following the title, and must appear in size of type no less than 50% the size of the largest letter of the title type.

EXTREMITIES was first produced in July 1980 by the Rutgers Theatre Company, directed by John Bettenbender; set design, Joseph F. Miklojcik, Jr.; costume design, Vickie Rita McLaughlin; lighting design, Kevin Holman; with the following cast:

MARJORIE	*Ellen Barber*
RAUL	*Danton Stone*
PATRICIA	*Mary Beth Fisher*
TERRY	*Catherine Schaeffer*

EXTREMITIES was produced in March 1981 at the Fifth Annual Festival of New American Plays at Actors Theatre of Louisville, Jon Jory, Artistic Director, directed by John Bettenbender; set design, Paul Owen; costume design, Kurt Wilhelm; lighting design, Jeff Hill; with the following cast:

MARJORIE	*Ellen Barber*
RAUL	*Danton Stone*
TERRY	*Peggity Price*
PATRICIA	*Kathy Bates*

EXTREMITIES represented the U.S.A. in the Baltimore International Festival in June 1981. The cast was the same as above with the exception of Giordana Rashovich, who played Marjorie.

The New York production opened at the Westside Arts Center, Cheryl Crawford Theatre, on December 22, 1982. Direction was by Robert Allan Ackerman; set design by Marjorie Bradley Kellogg; lighting design by Arden Fingerhut; costume design by Robert Wojewodski; action sequences by B. H. Barry; and sound design by Scott Lehrer. The cast, in order of appearance, was as follows:

MARJORIE	*Susan Sarandon*
RAUL	*James Russo*
TERRY	*Ellen Barkin*
PATRICIA	*Deborah Hedwall*

Produced on the New York stage by Gero Communications, Inc. and Della Koenig.

CAST

MARJORIE
RAUL
TERRY
PATRICIA

TIME — The present. September.

PLACE — Between Trenton and Princeton, New Jersey, where the cornfield meets the highway.

SET

The livingroom of an old farmhouse.
Dining table and three chairs.
Sofa and table.
A fireplace
A large window before which hang plants of every description
A door leading outside
A door leading to the kitchen
Stairs leading to other rooms in the house.
A locked bicycle against the wall.

Extremities

ACT ONE

SCENE 1

Bright sunlight through the window. Enter MAR-
JORIE in a bathrobe. She surveys the breakfast
dishes left on the table, sips a cup of tea. It's cold.
She puts on a large kettle of water. She makes a
phone call. No one answers apparently. She hangs
up. Don't rush the action. It's a lazy day. There are
no pressing priorities. She rises after noticing a wilted
plant. She touches it affectionately, sprays it with
water, rearranges it among the healthier plants. Still
not satisfied, she carries it out of the front door,
placing it on the outside sill. A wasp attacks her.
She swipes at it. The plant drops. We hear the pot-
tery crack. She is stung by the wasp

MARJORIE. Dammit to hell!

(She enters the house, slams the door closed. She
inspects the inner side of her thigh just above the
knee; two red circles. She bolts for a box of tools
near the plants. She finds an aerosol can of insec-
ticide. She shakes the can. She opens the door. An
unseen wasp hovering near the threshold makes her
give a little scream and slam the door closed. She
shakes the can. She opens the door quickly, sprays
the wasp, shakes the can, opens the door, sees no
wasp, opens the door wider, sees no wasp, opens
the door all the way, looks down, sees the dead
wasp. She kneels down to it. Pause. She sprays it

7

too much, takes a scoop shovel from the tool box,
scoops up the wasp, closes the door, drops the wasp
in the ashtray on the coffee table, sets the aerosol
can and shovel on the coffee table, sits, lights a
cigarette, takes one puff while studying the wasp,
glances at her stings, and without thought touches
the wasp with the cigarette. Enter RAUL.)

RAUL. Joe? Hey, Joe? It's me. O. How ya doin? Joe
in?

MARJORIE. (*rising quickly, tying her robe*) There's no
Joe here.

RAUL. He said he'd be in.

MARJORIE. No Joe lives here.

RAUL. O.

MARJORIE. You always just walk in people's houses?

RAUL. O, I'm sorry. Excuse me. I'm really sorry.

MARJORIE. It's ok.

RAUL. Have a good day.

MARJORIE. You too.

RAUL. Thank you very much.

MARJORIE. You're welcome.

RAUL. You live here?

MARJORIE. Good guess.

RAUL. What, Joe move out?

MARJORIE. Joe who?

RAUL. Joe—I forget.

MARJORIE. There never was any Joe here.

RAUL. What's this, all one house, or apartments?

MARJORIE. All one house.

RAUL. He said he had a room here.

MARJORIE. Apparently he lied.

RAUL. Yeah, him or somebody else.

MARJORIE. I'm sorry, you have to go.

RAUL. Can I use the phone, please?

MARJORIE. No, I'm sorry.

RAUL. It's a local call.

MARJORIE. No, you have to go.

RAUL. (*stroking the bicycle seat so gently*) You ride a bike?

MARJORIE. No, I use it to collect dust. There's the door.

RAUL. I know where the door is. You don't have to tell me where the door is. This is a real bitch. The guy owes me alotta money. Said come pick it up.

MARJORIE. Well there's no Joe here.

RAUL. You sure, sweetheart?

MARJORIE. Maybe my husband knows. He's upstairs.

RAUL. Why don't you ask him, babe?

MARJORIE. He's busy right now.

RAUL. Busy.

MARJORIE. Sleeping.

RAUL. Sleeping.

MARJORIE. He's a cop.

RAUL. No kidding?

MARJORIE. And I have to wake him up in five minutes for work.

RAUL. Shh! You might wake him up.

MARJORIE. You better go now.

RAUL. Cop, eh? Go ask him if he knows a guy named Joe.

MARJORIE. I told you he's sleeping.

RAUL. I dropped Joe off at this house last week.

MARJORIE. I think you have the wrong house.

RAUL. No. This house. He's about six two. Rides a Triumph. Red beard. Wears cowboy boots. Short guy.

MARJORIE. There's no guy here.

RAUL. Except the cop.

MARJORIE. Honey, come down here please?

RAUL. Boy, that cop's a sound sleeper.

MARJORIE. Honey?

RAUL. What's amatter?

MARJORIE. Honey.

RAUL. Just like a cop: never there when ya need 'em.

MARJORIE. Honey!

RAUL. Honey! Honey! What's amatter wit him?
Maybe he ain't here. Maybe you're tellin me alittle lie
eh, pretty momma? Maybe you think I scare easy. Go
'head. Go for the door. Let's see who's faster. So
where's the other two chicks that live here?

MARJORIE. Kitchen.

RAUL. House full of people, and when you hollar,
nobody comes. (*She bolts for the door; he cuts her
off.*)

MARJORIE. Get out!

RAUL. You got a lousy bunch of friends.

MARJORIE. Get out right now!

RAUL. Take it easy, lovely. I saw the other two chicks
leave this morning. The one wit the ratty car should get
here about five-thirty. The one wit specs, 'bout six. Today's gonna be a triple header.

MARJORIE. Get out!

(*Long pause. RAUL goes to door, looks at MAR-
JORIE, laughs, goes to phone, rips the wire out.*)

RAUL. Your move.

MARJORIE. I'm expecting people anytime now. Anytime.

RAUL. No kidding? Dressed like that? Mind if I stick
around for the fun? Your move.

MARJORIE. Don't touch me!

RAUL. Don't fight me. I don't want to hurt you. You're too sweet to hurt. Be nice. You smell pretty. Is that your smell or the perfume? Be nice. Wanna take a shower together first? I'll soap you up real good? Flip me alittle smile, babe. I'm gonna fuck you frontways, backways, sideways, and ways you never heard of. (*She runs. He latches onto her hair, brings her down, mounts her, forces a pillow to her face. We hear her muffled screams.*) You gonna be nice?

MARJORIE. (*muffled*) Yes!

RAUL. You sure?

MARJORIE. (*muffled*) Yes!

RAUL. (*removing the pillow slightly*) Please don't wreck it. You made me hurt you, and I don't want to hurt you, but if you kick and scream and scratch, what else can I do, eh, babe? (*She tries to escape once more; he subdues her with pillow.*) That pisses me off!

MARJORIE. (*muffled*) Please!

RAUL. See what you made me do!

MARJORIE. (*muffled*) Please don't!

RAUL. Want me to put out your light?

MARJORIE. (*muffled*) No!

RAUL. You gonna be nice?

MARJORIE. (*muffled*) Yes!

RAUL. What's that?

MARJORIE. (*muffled*) Yes! Yes!

RAUL. Heh?

MARJORIE. (*muffled*) Please don't kill me!

RAUL. Can't hear you.

MARJORIE. (*muffled*) Please! Don't kill me!

RAUL. If you're nice! Be nice! (*removing the pillow*) You don't want me to do it again, eh? (*shaking her head no*) Maybe you like to get hurt, eh? (*Shaking her head no. Pause. He smothers her again out of whim. She goes limp.*) Holy mother of god. A freckle. I didn't know you had freckles. I love freckles. I want to kiss 'em all. Give 'em names and kiss 'em all goodnight. Yeah. The first time I saw you I knew it was gonna be beautiful, but I didn't think this beautiful. I didn't think anything could be this beautiful . . . Not anything . . . Beautiful. (*He kisses her gently.*) Don't make your lips tight. They always make their lips tight. Do it nice. No. They're still tight. Kiss me nice. Yes. Yes. Nice. Smile. Smile! Nicer! How ya doin? Answer me!

MARJORIE. What?

RAUL. How ya doin? Say good.

MARJORIE. Good.

RAUL. Good. Invite me in.

MARJORIE. In where?

RAUL. Your house.

MARJORIE. We're already here.

RAUL. Nice place. Say thank you.

MARJORIE. Thank you.

RAUL. Kiss me and tell me you love me. Tell me!

MARJORIE. Please don't.

RAUL. Don't make it get ugly. Tell me you love me. Tell me!

MARJORIE. I love you.

RAUL. Say it nice.

MARJORIE. I love you.

RAUL. Tell me again and keep telling me.

MARJORIE. I love you I love you I love you . . .

RAUL. Yeah . . .

MARJORIE. I love you I love you I love you . . .

RAUL. More, more . . .

MARJORIE. I love you . . .

RAUL. How much?

MARJORIE. What?

RAUL. How much!

MARJORIE. How much what?

RAUL. You're trying to wreck this for me.

MARJORIE. No . . .

RAUL. Fuckin bitches always got to make it ugly!

MARJORIE. I love you!

RAUL. How much?

MARJORIE. Alot.

RAUL. More than what?

MARJORIE. I don't understand.

RAUL. You're gonna make me do something ugly.

MARJORIE. More than anything in the whole world! I love you!

RAUL. I love how you say that. Sweet.

MARJORIE. I love you.

RAUL. Touch me. All over. Nice. Again. Nicer. Touch my hair. My mouth. My neck. Keep telling me and don't stop.

MARJORIE. I love you I love you I love you . . .

RAUL. And keep touching me . . .

MARJORIE. I love you I love you . . .

RAUL. And touch me down there . . .

MARJORIE. I love you I love you . . .

RAUL. Touch me down there!

MARJORIE. I love you I love you . . .

RAUL. And tell me you wanna make love . . .

MARJORIE. I love you I love you . . .

RAUL. You're makin it ugly again!

MARJORIE. Please don't do this? Take anything you want. I've got jewelry upstairs.

RAUL. (*slapping her*) See! See! See what you made me do! Now touch me down there and say you wanna make love!

MARJORIE. I love you . . .

RAUL. And what else?

MARJORIE. I love you.

RAUL. Yeah, and what else?

MARJORIE. Make love.

RAUL. Who?

MARJORIE. You.

RAUL. And who else?

MARJORIE. Me.

RAUL. You wanna make love?

MARJORIE. Yes.

RAUL. Say it.

MARJORIE. I want to make love.

RAUL. You say that beautiful. Again.

MARJORIE. I want to make love.

RAUL. When?

MARJORIE. I don't know.

RAUL. Now?

MARJORIE. I don't know.

RAUL. This is your last chance.

MARJORIE. I love you and I want to make love.

RAUL. Scream.

MARJORIE. What?

RAUL. (*He clamps her leg just above the knee and squeezes.*) Scream! Louder! More! See? Nobody hears. Just me and you, puta. Say you're my puta.

MARJORIE. Puta?

RAUL. Puta, puta, whore, my whore, my puta! Say it!

MARJORIE. I'm your puta.

RAUL. Say it and smile!

MARJORIE. I'm your puta.

RAUL. You like to tease me, eh, puta?

MARJORIE. No. Yes. Yes.

RAUL. You like to tease everybody.

MARJORIE. No.

RAUL. Know what you need, puta? You need acouple slashes here and here and here, stripes t' make you a zebra-face t'scare the shit outta anybody you go teasin', puta, cause you're mine, all mine. Say it!

MARJORIE. Yours!

RAUL. Undo the belt.

MARJORIE. Please! God!

RAUL. Undo it! This is gonna be beautiful, so you keep telling me, puta, and don't stop . . .

MARJORIE. I love you, I love you . . .

RAUL. You smell so pretty . . .

MARJORIE. I love you . . .

RAUL. You put perfume on for me?

MARJORIE. (*seeing the aerosol almost in reach*) Yes!

RAUL. Just for me!

MARJORIE. (*reaching furtively, still too far*) Yes! Yes! I love you! I love you!

RAUL. You say that more and more beautiful!

MARJORIE. (*In order to reach the aerosol, she must embrace RAUL.*) I love you! I really really love you! I wanna be your puta!

RAUL. This is too beautiful!

MARJORIE. Yes!

RAUL. See! It don't have to be ugly, does it?

MARJORIE. No! No! Beautiful! I love you!

RAUL. I love when you hug me like that!

MARJORIE. I love you!

RAUL. Your perfume makes me drunk!

MARJORIE. I love you!

RAUL. You put it on for me?

MARJORIE. Yes!

RAUL. Just for me?

MARJORIE. (*grabs the can*) Just for you! (*Sprays his face. He screams, holds his eyes. MARJORIE pushes*

RAUL away with her foot and tries to run for the door but RAUL latches onto her leg. Struggling to escape, she yanks an extension cord from the socket, loops it around his neck and pulls. He screams.)

BLACKOUT

(*The sound of a wasp, or wasps, to cover the blackout.*)

SCENE 2

In the blackout RAUL's cry is more animal than human. Lights up slowly. RAUL is blindfolded and bound in a tangle of extension cords, clothesline, belts, and other household implements. He kicks and bucks and bites at his restraints. MARJORIE staggers to the sink. She turns on the water, splashes some on her face and wasp bite, turns on the kettle.

RAUL. You there? My eyes burn! I need a doctor! You there? I'm hurt bad! Help me! You there? Where are you? (*MARJORIE dials the phone.*) Call the cops, pussy! You can't prove a fuckin thing! (*Realizing the phone is dead, she drops it and watches RAUL buck.*) Why don't you fuckin answer me! You bitch! I'll kill ya! Get the cops! They gotta let me go! (*MARJORIE runs up the stairs.*) Your Honor, I goes out looking for work cause I got laid off the car wash and I sees this farmhouse and goes t'ask if there was any work cause I got three babies t'feed, and this crazy lady goes and sprays me with this stuff, Your Honor. (*MARJORIE rushes down the stairs holding her clothes in hand, opens the door, but stops upon the mention of her name.*) Go on, Marjorie, go down the road and stop a truck on the highway an tell 'em get the cops. You got no bruises, no witnesses, no come up your snatch. You got nothin, pussy. (*MARJORIE inadvertently lets the door slam.*) This is a civilized fuckin country, pussy! You don't go around tyin up innocent people, Marjorie!

MARJORIE. How do you know my name?

RAUL. I demand my rights! I want medical attention! I wanna call my attorney! Palmieri! The fuckin best!

MARJORIE. How do you know my name?

RAUL. And when you're alone in the room wit the pigs and tell 'em what happened, and they say, You sure, sweetheart? They don't believe no pricktease, Marjorie.

MARJORIE. Don't say my name.

RAUL. And little Margie gets a little write-up in the paper and wit Daddy's heart condition that could be real sweet if the old fucker croaks . . .

MARJORIE. My father?

RAUL. And me, I'm sippin o.j. in some nice clean hospital bed jawin with the candy-stripers and every freako-scuz-fuck and happy headhunter who rake the papers for hits come pussy-sniffin out here like a pack o junkyard dogs after a bitch in heat and maybe drop in unannounced for a wet dick . . . (*The tea kettle begins to whistle.*) What's that! Siren? You call the cops? (*MARJORIE gets the kettle. We must see the steam.*) You don't got a fuckin case! They gotta miranda me! and let me go! (*MARJORIE is about to return the kettle.*) And then one day I come back . . . (*She stops.*) Get you in some parking lot and carve up that teasin face . . .

MARJORIE. No!

RAUL. Who the fuck you think you're playin wit,

bitch? (*MARJORIE snaps and dumps hot water on him. He screams. She screams.*)

BLACKOUT

(*The sound of wasps cover the blackout.*)

SCENE 3

Lights up slowly. RAUL is in the fireplace. MARJORIE has lashed the bicycle to the fireplace. It is locked with the bicycle chain.

RAUL. Where am I? Marjorie? Where am I?

MARJORIE. How do you know my name?

RAUL. Where am I?

MARJORIE. (*tugging his noose*) Answer me.

RAUL. I can't talk! Marjorie!

MARJORIE. Don't you ever say my name again! How'd you know me?

RAUL. I read it on a letter.

MARJORIE. (*tugging his noose*) What letter?

RAUL. Heartless bitch!

MARJORIE. What letter?

RAUL. I took some letters from your mailbox by mistake. This guy Joe asked me to come pick up his mail.

MARJORIE. Who were the letters from?

RAUL. One from your father. One from a collection agency. A couple from guys.

MARJORIE. Who?

RAUL. Some guy Tony. He wants you come live with him in New York. He don't want you to tell Terry.

MARJORIE. Who else?

RAUL. Your brother in Marine boot camp. Says they're beatin the shit outta him down there. He thinks he's got it bad.

MARJORIE. Why me? Answer me. Why me?

RAUL. Don't know. Crazy whacko bitch! What the hell!

MARJORIE. Why me?

RAUL. I saw you around.

MARJORIE. Where?

RAUL. Around! I don't know! Please! (*She pokes him with a fireplace implement.*)

MARJORIE. Answer me!

RAUL. I don't know what to say!

MARJORIE. Try the truth!

RAUL. O, the truth! Why didn't you say so! Alright! Here it goes. The truth. This guy Joe . . . (*She pokes him.*) That's the truth! I swear on my mother's grave! Whattaya nuts or what! You said the truth, I told the truth, and you go poke me! (*She stops poking.*) You wanna hear this or not?

MARJORIE. Go ahead.

RAUL. You won't poke me?

MARJORIE. I said go ahead!

RAUL. Alright. The truth. There was this guy Joe . . . (*He flinches in anticipation of a poke.*) He's a pimp. Said for half a yard he'd fix me up with a knock-out pussy. Said walk right in and ask for him and you'd know what I meant but I guess he was playing a joke on me. (*She pokes him.*)

RAUL. Please! Stop! Marjorie!

MARJORIE. Don't say my name!

RAUL. You are the boss, Jack! You are the man! Whatever you say! Ok? No panic. Listen, can I ask you one little question, Marjorie? — It slipped! I swear on my grandmother's milk! — One little question. Where am I?

MARJORIE. Fireplace.

RAUL. Where?

MARJORIE. The fireplace.

RAUL. What for?

MARJORIE. Why do people put things in the fireplace?

RAUL. People put things in the fire . . . (*pause*) Hey, c'mon, don't joke around.

MARJORIE. (*shaking a plastic bottle of ammonia*) And I have some gas.

RAUL. Gas? What, for your car?

MARJORIE. No. For you.

RAUL. I don't even own a car.

MARJORIE. (*shaking a box of wooden matches*) And matches.

RAUL. Whoa, jack! — Listen, I been doin some deep thinkin here and now I'm ready for the truth. I mean the real truth. I'm a narco. We got a tip there was drugs in this house. Open up. I'll show you my badge. (*She douses him with ammonia.*) Hey! What the hell! Hey! I got a wife and three kids!

MARJORIE. (*striking a match very near*) Maybe you'll tell the truth when you're on fire! (*RAUL coughs uncontrollably. He fights for breath in the chemicalized air. MARJORIE strikes a match, holds it close to his face.*)

RAUL. Alright! This is it! The honest-to-god truth. I don't know why I didn't tell you this from the beginning because this is it. (*pause*) I used to work on the pothole crew. For the County. We went around patchin up potholes. One day we was patchin up potholes on the highway. In front of your driveway. Bitchin day. In the nineties. Working with hot tar. Sweatin. Thirsty. Gettin dizzy. Foreman bustin balls. Somebody says, look at this. And you come ridin down the highway on your bike in your little white shorts and everytime you pedal you could see what was tan and what wasn't and your blouse tied in a knot and the sun shinin off your hair, beautiful. And that's it.

MARJORIE. So why'd you come here?

RAUL. I just told you. You was beautiful.

MARJORIE. So what?

RAUL. You know what that does to a man. It was hot. You had on your little white shorts.

MARJORIE. You're gonna burn. (*MARJORIE flicks matches wildly.*)

RAUL. Please! We had a deal! On the milk of Mary! You rode by in your shorts! I said How ya doin? You didn't say nothing. Looked at me like I was a dead dog. You pissed me off so I came back here to fuck you! (*MARJORIE stops flicking matches. RAUL whimpers and slumps down. MARJORIE sits. Long pause.*) You there? (*pause*) Whattaya gonna do wit me?

MARJORIE. (*Pause. With perfect aplomb:*) Nothing.

RAUL. Nothing?

MARJORIE. Nothing.

RAUL. You mean—let me go?

MARJORIE. No. Nothing.

RAUL. I don't catch what you're talkin.

MARJORIE. (*silence*) You will.

RAUL. When?

MARJORIE. You'll see.

RAUL. Starve me?

MARJORIE. Good idea.

RAUL. You could get the chair for that? Why don't you just call the cops?

MARJORIE. Why should I?

RAUL. That's what they're there for! (*pause*)

MARJORIE. Two days. No food. No water.

RAUL. You can't do this!

MARJORIE. I am doing it.

RAUL. I really think you should call the cops.

MARJORIE. You said I have no proof, they'll let you go.

RAUL. No. Marjorie, I swear, I was just talkin. Get the cops.

MARJORIE. It's too late.

RAUL. Mother of god! I don't want to die like this! Answer me! Talk to me! Please! — What will you do wit, you know, my body?

MARJORIE. Bury it.

RAUL. Bury it?

MARJORIE. I started a graveyard near the woods for the animals that get killed up on the highway. This time I dig deeper.

RAUL. You're jerkin me off.

MARJORIE. I got a shovel.

RAUL. Don't shit around! I got a weak ticker! (*pause*) My wife's eight months pregnant. She won't let me touch her. I'm goin nuts. I got to get it everyday. I need help. Honest to fuckin god. I want to go straight.

MARJORIE. You will. Straight in a fuckin hole.

RAUL. You ain't got the nuts, cunt.

MARJORIE. You say that when you're in the bottom of the hole and the first shovel of dirt hits you in the face!

RAUL. When they come home, the other chicks, they'll stop you!

MARJORIE. You think so? One helps me dig the hole, the other helps me drag you out!

RAUL. You can't do this!

MARJORIE. I want to hear you scream under the dirt,

like me under the pillow. (*exit for a shovel*)

RAUL. Mother of god!

MARJORIE. And you suck in for air, and dirt fills your mouth and nose!

RAUL. Send me your angel, mother of god!

MARJORIE. Suck for air! Under the dirt! with possum skulls! and dog bones!

RAUL. Get the cops! I want to tell 'em everything! This is it! (*MARJORIE pretends to leave by slamming the door.*) Marjorie! Marjorie! Marjorie! — She's diggin the hole, diggin the hole, she's really diggin the hole! (*pause*) O mother of god, do the miracle! Break these chains! (*He tries.*) Break these bars! (*He tries.*) What's amatter? Send me an angel like before! How can you let me die like this? (*Pause. Singing.*)

Found a peanut
It was rotten
Ate it anyway just now
Then I died
Went to heaven . . .

(*pause*) What I do this time? What I do? I didn't do nothin. (*Pause. Singing.*)

Broke the statue
Knocked it over
Broke the Virgin just now
Got a beatin
Locked the closet
Wit the spiders just now.

(*pause*) You there? I know you're there, Marjorie. Please be there. How can you just sit there after alls between us? How can you do this to me? (*He thrashes about, gags, falls down, becomes still.*)

MARJORIE. Is it too tight? You alright? (*No answer. Pause. She probes him with the shovel, nothin. MAR-*

JORIE reaches to loosen the noose. RAUL bites her hand. She screams, cries, picks up the stick, but getting a better idea, hurls it at the cage, storms the kitchen.)
RAUL.
Bit the big bitch!
Bit the big bitch!
Bit the big bitch just now!
She was rotten!
Rotten! rotten!
La la la la! la la!

(MARJORIE enters running with the plastic container of Clorox and douses him.)

RAUL. *(continued)* I'm on fire! I'm good! I'm good! I'm gonna learn to tell the truth! the whole truth! nothin but the truth! I swear to fuckin god! Car! Car! Please, mother of god, let it be the cops!
MARJORIE. *(pulling him against bars by noose)* Talk again and I smash you like a fuckin bug!

(MARJORIE looks out the window, sees TERRY with full arms, opens the door. Enter TERRY with grocery bags.)

TERRY. What a day! *(Exit TERRY in the kitchen.)* That guy Danny I told you about? He cornered me by the water cooler and said, I'm taking you out to dinner tonight and not taking no for an answer, so I can't help you guys scrape and paint tonight, and look, Margie honey sweet lovely cutie-pie good friend, can I borrow your red dress, the one with the spaghetti straps and slit up the . . . *(discovering Raul)* There's a man in the fireplace.

MARJORIE. Don't get scared. He tried to rape me.

TERRY. O Mother Mary.

MARJORIE. He's been watching us. He knows all about us, when you work, when you come home, when Pat comes home, our cars, everything.

TERRY. Who is he?

RAUL. Please help me! She hurt me bad!

MARJORIE. (*poking him*) What'd I say about talking?

RAUL. Not to!

MARJORIE. And what'd you do?

RAUL. I talked.

MARJORIE. And what do you deserve?

RAUL. Help me!

MARJORIE. What do you deserve?

RAUL. The stick. (*She hurts him, he screams.*)

TERRY. Marjorie! It's over now! We'll get the police and lock him up!

MARJORIE. On what charge?

TERRY. Rape.

MARJORIE. There was no rape.

TERRY. Attempted rape.

MARJORIE. Prove it. (*pause*) You can't. So they let him go and he said he'd come back to get me. So it's him or me. Him or me. Choose. Him or me.

TERRY. I'd rather call the police.

MARJORIE. Do it.

TERRY. It would make me feel safe.

MARJORIE. Then do it.

TERRY. What should I say?

MARJORIE. Whatever makes you feel safe.

TERRY. Phone's dead.

MARJORIE. Animal ripped it out of the wall. I got lucky. If I didn't you would've come home and found my body . . .

TERRY. Don't talk like that.

MARJORIE. You try and run. He catches you by the hair. Smothers you off and on till you're too weak to move.

TERRY. Alright!

MARJORIE. And then he toys with you. Makes you beg for a breath. Makes you undo his belt.

TERRY. Stop it!

MARJORIE. Makes you touch him. All over. His mouth. His neck. Between his legs . . .

TERRY. Why are you doing this to me!

MARJORIE. So it won't happen to you! — Terry, if it happened to you, I'd say, Terry, tell me what to do.

TERRY. Tell me what to do.

MARJORIE. Be with me.

TERRY. I am with you. (*pause*) What can I do?

MARJORIE. Help me make him disappear.

TERRY. Let's wait for Pat.

MARJORIE. We don't need her. We only need the shovel.

TERRY. Shovel?

MARJORIE. To dig a hole in the garden.

TERRY. Hole?

MARJORIE. And that's the end of it.

TERRY. O God.

MARJORIE. Him or us. Choose. Say him and I open the cage and let him go. But if he gets you, don't blame me because you chose him. So decide now. Him or us. (*pause*) Decide! (*pause*) Say it. Him or us.

TERRY. Us.

MARJORIE. Good. Just dig the hole. I'll do the rest.

TERRY. Don't let me see it, alright?

MARJORIE. See what?

TERRY. The blood.

MARJORIE. What blood? We drag him out, throw him in the hole, and cover it up.

TERRY. O God.

MARJORIE. Is the world better or worse without him?

TERRY. I don't want to touch him.

MARJORIE. Alright, I can drag him myself. You just dig the hole. (*TERRY takes the shovel.*) Dig between the tomatoes and the flowerbed. The ground's soft there.

TERRY. I'd rather you dig.

MARJORIE. Then you watch.

TERRY. I'd rather you watch.

MARJORIE. I can't do both.

TERRY. You dig.

MARJORIE. Then watch him and don't leave the room.

TERRY. Marjorie? Let's think about this some more?

MARJORIE. What's to think about? It's simple. Him or you. Choose. (*Pause. TERRY sits. Exit MARJORIE with shovel.*)

RAUL. Pst! Pst!

TERRY. Be quiet, please.

RAUL. She gone? Is she?

TERRY. Yes.

RAUL. C'mer. C'mer.

TERRY. You will have to not talk.

RAUL. Terry, I need help. She sprayed me with stuff. My eyes're killin me! Please help me. I'm serious.

TERRY. Just shut up.

RAUL. So you're gonna help whacko poof me, eh?

TERRY. You better not let her catch you talking.

RAUL. Terry, Terry, my Good Humor truck broke down on the highway. I wanted to call the office before the ice cream melted. I just asked to use the phone . . .

TERRY. I'll tell her you talked.

RAUL. Then share the crime. It's called complicity. That means you sit there like an asshole and watch somebody do a crime.

TERRY. Look, I'm not interested in what you have to say.

RAUL. How about my attorney? Interested in what he has to say? eh? when you're up in that witness chair? in front of the Big Twelve? and he goes, Tell the court what you did, Terry, when whacko was diggin the hole and my client was sufferin terrible and begged you open the cage? And Terry says, Nothin, and His Honor hits ya wit Croak One, and you go the iron Hyatt. The wall. So you gonna open this up or not? (*pause*) Ok, asshole. The wall. Ever hear of my attorney? Palmieri?

TERRY. Yes.

RAUL. The best, right? (*He takes her silence for consent.*) For two g's the man walks on water, so think about it, jailbird. Open it, Terry—you don't want no record. (*pause*) Ok. Palmieri. Complicity. The wall. (*TERRY pours herself a glass of wine; at these sounds:*) Can I have alittle swig of that? Parched from screaming. (*pause*) Hang it up, jailbird! You ride with whacko! The wall. Know about the wall? Nooooooo-oooooo. Jailbird don't know diddly shit bout no wall. That why you sit there doin complicity when you could be givin me alittle swig o juice so's I could tell Palmieri, Lay off the chick Terry, she's alright, she did what she could. (*pause*) Not even that, eh? (*pause*) Now I know how Christ felt. (*pause*) Whattaya say at confession this week? eh, Terry? Bless me father for I have sinned. I buried the Good Humor man. Ain't goin over too big, Terry. What do you think father's gonna say? say three hail Mary's and don't do it again? The fucker'll break out handcuffs on the spot! But I understand. You're doin it for Marjorie, good friend Marjorie.

TERRY. Will you shut up?

RAUL. Tight with Marjorie, eh? Friends to the ends,

eh? You borrow her dress, she borrows your boyfriend. (*pause*) Tony.

TERRY. What?

RAUL. Forget it.

TERRY. No. What did you say?

RAUL. O, you want something from me, but when I ask you for alittle drink, you gimme a cup o dust. Get lost, you and your fuckin drink.

TERRY. You're a goddamn liar.

RAUL. Am I?

TERRY. What'd she say?

RAUL. Don't believe me. I'm a liar. Go believe your good friend out there diggin a hole. She's nice. She burries people.

TERRY. What'd she tell you?

RAUL. Look, nobody like to be the one to bring the bad news. (*pause*) She's fuckin' him.

TERRY. He doesn't even live round here anymore!

RAUL. New York. (*pause*) Photographer. (*pause*) She goes see him every Wednesday. You drop her off the train station. (*pause*) Think what you're doin, Terry. She get raped? She got broken bones? I pinched her ass, she took a freak and mangled me. Ever get your ass pinched? Course you did. Did you mangle the guy? Course not. Think, sweetheart, think.

TERRY. Tell me everything she said.

RAUL. Just wet my lips alittle? please?

TERRY. Alright.

RAUL. Thank you so much. I want to light a candle for you. God bless you . . . (*He latches onto her wrist.*) You scream and I bite your hand the fuck off.

TERRY. Please don't hurt me!

RAUL. I'm not that type person, babe. Undo the lock. (*TERRY blows her rape whistle.*) You fuckin asshole!

You fucked yourself real good! They're gonna eat you alive at the wall!

(*Enter MARJORIE. RAUL releases TERRY's hand.*)

MARJORIE. What happened?

RAUL. Marjorie! I'm sorry! She gave me a drink of wine.

MARJORIE. Why?

TERRY. I did not!

RAUL. How'd the glass get in here?

MARJORIE. Goddamit (*MARJORIE bangs the fire-screen with the shovel.*)

TERRY. I'm leaving!

MARJORIE. What'd he say?

TERRY. Where are my keys?

MARJORIE. The hole's half dug!

TERRY. I don't care.

MARJORIE. We're halfway there!

TERRY. Move.

MARJORIE. You said you would help me.

TERRY. I don't care what I said.

MARJORIE. Why can't you help me?

TERRY. I don't know what happened here and I don't care. You're alive. So what's it matter? Just get him out of this house.

(*Sound of a car. Enter PATRICIA with briefcase and bakery box tied up neatly with a string.*)

PATRICIA. What's up with you broads? — Look, cherry cheesecake! — Did somebody die on the soaps? (*RAUL rattles his cage. Pause. PATRICIA laughs.*)

Ok, what's the joke? C'mon, c'mon you *guys!* I'm not falling for this one! Who's that?

TERRY. He tried to rape Marjorie.

PATRICIA. O, dear. (*pause*) You ok?

MARJORIE. I think so.

PATRICIA. Are you?

MARJORIE. Yes.

PATRICIA. How'd he get like that?

MARJORIE. I did it.

PATRICIA. You?

MARJORIE. Yes.

PATRICIA. Alone?

MARJORIE. Yes.

PATRICIA. And you're ok?

MARJORIE. Yes.

PATRICIA. When?

MARJORIE. Before—an hour—two—I don't know.

PATRICIA. Where's the police? Did you call?

MARJORIE. No.

PATRICIA. Why not?

MARJORIE. I'm going to fix him.

PATRICIA. Fix?

MARJORIE. Fix.

RAUL. Don't let her torture me no more!

MARJORIE. Shut the fuck up!

PATRICIA. What are you doing?

MARJORIE. I want him to hurt like me!

RAUL. Please help me.

PATRICIA. Stop it!

MARJORIE. I want him to hurt like me!

PATRICIA. Looks like you've done that. Now we have to put him away.

MARJORIE. I have no proof! They'll let him go! He'll come back and slash up my face!

PATRICIA. The fact that he's on the premises should put him away.

MARJORIE. Is that true?

PATRICIA. Honest. Honest. (*pause, disarming her gently*) It's going to be alright, honest. We'll take care of everything. You relax. Lie down. There. There. Yes. Here is a nice pillow . . .

MARJORIE. No!

PATRICIA. Ok. Everything is fine. Terry, would you call?

TERRY. Phone's dead.

PATRICIA. Ok. Would you get the police?

TERRY. What do I say?

PATRICIA. Tell them to come quickly.

TERRY. What do we say about him?

PATRICIA. Tell them to come and take him away.

TERRY. No, I mean if they see him like that, she's in trouble.

MARJORIE. What kind of trouble?

TERRY. Big trouble.

RAUL. A&B, mayhem, AD&W.

MARJORIE. Is that true?

PATRICIA. We'll get a lawyer.

MARJORIE. Lawyer?

TERRY. You have to, Marjorie.

PATRICIA. For your protection.

TERRY. They'll crucify you.

PATRICIA. Terry, please.

TERRY. We better get a lawyer before we get the police.

PATRICIA. You don't need a lawyer. The state prosecutes. You're only a witness.

MARJORIE. I want a lawyer.

PATRICIA. Ok. Look in the phonebook under P for Palmieri.

TERRY. Holy shit.

PATRICIA. What?

TERRY. That's his lawyer.

PATRICIA. How do you know?

TERRY. He told me.

MARJORIE. You talked with him?

PATRICIA. We'll take care of everything.

TERRY. I think we should make up a story.

PATRICIA. What?

TERRY. I'll say I was with Marjorie when he broke in.

PATRICIA. That's perjury.

TERRY. If it comes to his word against hers, he wins.

PATRICIA. We tell the truth. Now will you please hurry?

TERRY. You know his lawyer's going to file counter-charges and haul her downtown.

MARJORIE. Is that true?

PATRICIA. It's just a formality.

TERRY. That's all. But bring a toothbrush.

PATRICIA. Don't worry about jail.

MARJORIE. Jail!

TERRY. Listen! Me and Marjorie are watching t.v., animal breaks in, there's a struggle, we hogtie him, he resists, we're afraid he'll escape, we stuff him in the fireplace, and went for the police.

MARJORIE. Police. Charges. Arraignment. Lawyers. Money. Time. Judge. Jury. Proof. His word against mine. Defendant's attorney — a three-piece button down summa cum laude fresh from Harvard fuck-off: Did my client rape you? No. Assault you? Yes. How? With a pillow. Did you resist? Yes. Evidence? None. Witnesses? None. Did you tie him up? beat him? lock him in a fireplace? Six months for me, that animal goes free. And if I survive being locked up, then what do I do? Come home and lock myself up. Chainlock, boltlock, deadlock. And wait for him. Hear him in every creak of wood, every mouse in the wall, every twig tapping on the window. Start from sleep, 4 A.M. see something in the dark at the foot of my bed. Eyes black holes. Skin speckled gray like a slug. Hit the lights. He's not there. This time. So then what do I do? Wait for him? Or move three thousand miles, change my name, unlist my phone, get a dog. I don't want to taste my vomit everytime the doorbell rings. I don't want to flinch when a man touches me. I won't wear a goddamn whistle. I want to live my life. He's never leaving this house.

PATRICIA. (*pause*) Marjorie I think you're in shock and don't know what you're saying. I'm going to a phonebooth and call the police and everything's going to be alright.

MARJORIE. I'm not in shock, and more than ever I know exactly what I'm saying, and you're not going anywhere. (*snatching up their car keys*)

PATRICIA. My keys, please.

MARJORIE. No.

PATRICIA. Then I guess we'll have to walk. (*MARJORIE takes a claw hammer from a toolbox near the door.*)

MARJORIE. You leave this house, animal dies.

PATRICIA. O, Marjorie, you don't really mean that.

RAUL. She means it! Please don't leave me!

MARJORIE. From now on, I make my own law. (*She locks the door. PATRICIA and TERRY sit.*)

RAUL. Mother of god. (*Lights fade.*)

END OF ACT ONE

ACT TWO

Scene 1

The same as end of Act One. Lights up quickly.

PATRICIA. Ok, everything's fine. (*MARJORIE barricades door.*) Let's relax now and sit down and talk.

MARJORIE. I'm done talking.

PATRICIA. Ok, let's have a drink and some food.

MARJORIE. You eat.

PATRICIA. Ok, I'll open some wine. (*Exit PATRICIA to kitchen.*)

MARJORIE. What are you doing!

PATRICIA. I just opened the window.

MARJORIE. Close it!

PATRICIA. Ok.

MARJORIE. Lock it!

PATRICIA. Ok. (*MARJORIE runs around locking the windows.*)

RAUL. Thank you, Terry.

MARJORIE. What? (*pause*) Thank you for what?

TERRY. I don't know.

MARJORIE. What'd you say?

RAUL. Thank you.

MARJORIE. For what?

RAUL. Not you.

MARJORIE. Thank you for what?

RAUL. To Terry.

MARJORIE. For what? (*MARJORIE jerks the noose.*)

RAUL. Please, I can't breathe!

MARJORIE. Thank you for what!

RAUL. For making the noose looser.

MARJORIE. Goddamit!

TERRY. Pat, did I move from this chair?

MARJORIE. You keep away from the animal!

TERRY. Marjorie, I never went near him!

MARJORIE. Do you understand that!

PATRICIA. Terry! please!

TERRY. Sonofabitch!

MARJORIE. No more!

PATRICIA. Let's calm the hell down, please! everyone!

MARJORIE. Where do you think you're going?

TERRY. My room.

MARJORIE. Stay here.

TERRY. Why?

MARJORIE. I said so. Sit down. Now. (*TERRY sits.*)

RAUL. God bless you, Terry.

MARJORIE. Shut up!

PATRICIA. Ok, Ok, Terry, would you please fix something to eat? Please? Cold cuts and cheese. Put it on a plate and bring in some bread.

TERRY. Let's send for a pizza.

PATRICIA. Terry! — Please? (*Exit TERRY to kitchen.*)

PATRICIA. Wine?

MARJORIE. You know wine makes me sleepy. — Or is that what you want?

PATRICIA. Coffee?

MARJORIE. No.

PATRICIA. Anything?

MARJORIE. Silence. Thank you. (*pause*)

PATRICIA. (*touching MARJORIE who doesn't respond*) You're welcome. (*pause*) Sweater?

MARJORIE. I'm hot.

PATRICIA. You're shivering.

MARJORIE. I have to go to the bathroom.

PATRICIA. Well — go. O. Ok. You want me to go with you?

MARJORIE. That guy you were supposed to see tonight, does he know where you live?

TERRY. No. Yes. I think.

MARJORIE. Does he or not?

TERRY. Yes.

MARJORIE. Would he come here to see why you stood him up?

TERRY. How should I know?

MARJORIE. What do you think?

TERRY. Maybe. He'd call first.

MARJORIE. If he calls with the phone broke, what would he hear?

TERRY. Busy signal.

PATRICIA. He'd just hear dead air. Nothing.

TERRY. Or a recording: The number you have reached is being held hostage.

PATRICIA. Ok, Terry! — I'll call the phone company from work tomorrow.

MARJORIE. Tomorrow. You both have to take the day off tomorrow.

TERRY. Bullshit.

PATRICIA. Marjorie, tomorrow's staff meeting.

MARJORIE. I'm sorry.

TERRY. I used all my sick days. One more and I'm fired.

MARJORIE. Tough shit.

PATRICIA. Let it go.

TERRY. You let it go. I'm talking to you. One more thing and I'm fired. Then I could be like you and polish my nails and read glamour magazines all day.

PATRICIA. Terry.

TERRY. Patricia!

MARJORIE. If he comes here, I want you in the kitchen until I get rid of him. Do you understand?

TERRY. Your wish, Ayatollah. (*Exit TERRY to kitchen. TERRY brings in food, pours wine, hands one to MARJORIE, who doesn't take it.*)

TERRY. Wine? (*pause*) So what'd you do in the City yesterday? (*pause*)

PATRICIA. Ok, let's just eat now? Sandwich?

TERRY. Roastbeef's dry.

PATRICIA. Somebody didn't seal it properly. (*RAUL moans.*)

PATRICIA. I can't eat with him in there. (*PATRICIA lights a cigarette. Upon hearing the match struck:*)

RAUL. Please don't burn me again!

PATRICIA. Burn you? I only lit a cigarette.

RAUL. O, it's you, the nice one. I thought it was, you-know-who. She said she was gonna burn me alive. She dumped gas on me!

MARJORIE. It was only ammonia.

RAUL. And she flicked matches at me!

TERRY. I don't believe it! (*RAUL throws a few matches out in front of the fireplace. PATRICIA picks them up.*)

TERRY. How could you do that?

MARJORIE. No more talking with the animal!

PATRICIA. Why not?

MARJORIE. Because he's mine and I say you can't. (*PATRICIA drops the matches on the table and then takes a plate, puts some food on it, brings it towards the fireplace.*)

MARJORIE. What's that?

PATRICIA. He must be hungry.

RAUL. I am! (*MARJORIE bangs the firescreen with hammer.*) I'm not.

PATRICIA. Let me remind you, — he's a human being like you or me.

MARJORIE. Don't include me in any of the social theories you learned from a book.

PATRICIA. I wouldn't think of going over your head.

MARJORIE. So, what's your analysis? Is it his childhood? His environment? his Greek traumas? Let's hear the dimestore psychiatrist explain this sick creep animal fuck.

PATRICIA. Exactly who is the animal here is not entirely clear to me.

MARJORIE. Is this clear? Don't mess with the animals.

PATRICIA. Nobody dies in my house. (*PATRICIA and TERRY sit. Long pause.*)

RAUL. Excuse me.

MARJORIE. Shut your face, animal.

RAUL. Can I talk to Patti?

MARJORIE. Don't call anyone's name as if you knew us!

PATRICIA. What do you want?

RAUL. Me?

PATRICIA. Yes. — What's your name?

MARJORIE. NO! Say it, animal, and I smash your head.

PATRICIA. Why can't he say his name?

MARJORIE. Because if I hear it I'll put him under!

PATRICIA. Ok. What'd you want to tell me?

RAUL. Can I have a little glass of water please? My throat . . .

MARJORIE. No.

RAUL. I feel sick.

PATRICIA. What kind of sick?

RAUL. Bad sick. Dizzy. Headache. My eyes burn bad. She sprayed that stuff in my mouth.

PATRICIA. What stuff?

RAUL. I'm holdin my vomit because I didn't want to, you know, mess up the place.

PATRICIA. (*reading the aerosol can*) "Harmful or

fatal if swallowed. Harmful if inhaled or absorbed through skin. Get immediate medical attention. Atrophine is antidotal."

RAUL. What's that mean?

PATRICIA. "Do not spray toward face. Avoid breathing spray mist. Do not apply to humans, pets, dishes, or utensils. Keep out of reach of children." What's wrong?

RAUL. Nothin.

PATRICIA. Why are you gagging?

RAUL. I feel like, I don't know, like I absorbed something through my skin.

PATRICIA. I would like to go to the drugstore and get the atrophine.

MARJORIE. No.

PATRICIA. This stuff could be fatal. (*putting the can on the table, next to the matches*)

MARJORIE. No.

PATRICIA. Then what exactly are your intentions?

MARJORIE. What?

PATRICIA. What are you going to do with him?

MARJORIE. I don't know.

PATRICIA. Ok, you don't know. Thank you for being honest.

MARJORIE. Hey, look, I'm not one of your fuckin socialworker cases.

PATRICIA. Ok.

MARJORIE. So don't come off with this superior bullshit.

PATRICIA. Ok.

MARJORIE. And don't run your routine over me.

PATRICIA. Ok, ok, relax.

MARJORIE. I don't want to relax.

PATRICIA. Ok, then we've established you don't want

to relax and you've admitted you don't know your intentions.

MARJORIE. I didn't "admit" it. I said it.

PATRICIA. Ok, you said it.

MARJORIE. I didn't admit it like it was a crime. I said it.

PATRICIA. Ok, it was a poor choice of words on my part. I'll be more careful. Now, how do you feel about your situation?

MARJORIE. Wonderful. I think it should happen to everyone.

PATRICIA. Sarcasm won't help assess the reality of the problem.

MARJORIE. Fuck reality.

PATRICIA. And the reality is — a man is hurt and you don't have a case.

MARJORIE. That's why I have a hammer.

PATRICIA. Ok, you have a hammer. Let's talk about the hammer.

MARJORIE. My favorite subject. Hammer. One good swing can do more than judge, jury, and prosecutor! (*She whacks a plate on the table.*)

PATRICIA. Ok, let's define our terms. What do you want from him?

MARJORIE. A confession.

PATRICIA. Good.

MARJORIE. In front of you both.

PATRICIA. Excellent.

MARJORIE. To protect me from the law.

PATRICIA. Wonderful.

MARJORIE. What happened today fact for fact.

PATRICIA. Ok, that's something solid.

RAUL. I didn't do nothin.

PATRICIA. This is your chance to save yourself.

RAUL. I didn't do nothin, Patti.

PATRICIA. She's giving you a chance.

RAUL. Chance for what? Go the wall for a bit I didn't pull? Thanks.

MARJORIE. You tell them what you did to me.

RAUL. Look at her and look at me. Who did what to who?

MARJORIE. Tell them. Please?

RAUL. I wanna call my attorney. I want my rights. This country's got a fuckin constitution!

MARJORIE. Tell them how you smothered me.

RAUL. This land got laws, jack, and nobody's above the law!

MARJORIE. You made me touch you!

TERRY. Pat! Do something!

MARJORIE. Tell them. Please. Let's end it.

RAUL. No innocent person's got nothin to fear in this country. I demand my fuckin rights! (*MARJORIE bangs RAUL's hand with the hammer. He screams.*)

MARJORIE. If you knew what it was like under the pillow, sucking for breath that wasn't there.

PATRICIA. Tell me—talk about the pillow.

MARJORIE. Talk, hell, let me show you. (*forcing a pillow to PATRICIA's face*)

PATRICIA. Get the hell away from me with that thing!

MARJORIE. This is not a thing! This is a pillow! Let's define our terms!

PATRICIA. It'll all come out in court!

MARJORIE. Before they belive a woman in court, she has to be dead on arrival!

PATRICIA. You are not the law! You are not God! You have to bring it to court!

TERRY. We can't just keep him like a pet.

PATRICIA. Why don't you shut the hell up!

MARJORIE. Yeah! You're interrupting Patricia's routine!

PATRICIA. I hope we can rise above this personal bullshit.

MARJORIE. It's very personal. It's between me and him. So keep out of it.

PATRICIA. When will you be satisfied? When you become like him?

MARJORIE. Like him? I crave to be like him! No mind, no care, nothing human holding back the impulse to strike, tear, slash, and reduce him to splinters of bone! O God, make me more like him! Don't stare at me! Forgive me for surviving. Maybe you'd care more if you came home and tripped over my body and found animal waiting for you! What's going on here! Don't I count? What about me? Don't I count?

PATRICIA. I'm sorry. If we have to take off tomorrow, we take off. We're going to do the best thing for Marjorie.

RAUL. Burn. One, two, three.

PATRICIA. Ok. Let's relax. Wine? O, forgot. Ok. Now I'm sure the three of us can come up with something positive.

TERRY. This has nothing to do with me.

PATRICIA. I can understand how you feel.

TERRY. No you can't . . . Only I understand how I feel.

PATRICIA. Ok, I can relate to that.

TERRY. And I'm not taking off tomorrow, because you're not worth it.

PATRICIA. Ok, Terry seems to feel alienated. Ok. Let's look at the facts. We got a man here. He's tied up. He's injured. What does this mean? God, I can't think today. Ok. The problem is this: what laws are violated? Do we all agree on what the problem is? (*pause*) Ok, let's stick with the facts. Do you have any bruises?

MARJORIE. He bit me.

PATRICIA. Wonderful! — I mean, you know, for court. It shows.

RAUL. She's right, Patti. I bit her because she was chokin me with a wire!

PATRICIA. Did you put anything on it?

MARJORIE. Peroxide.

PATRICIA. Ok. What's with your leg?

MARJORIE. I got stung. Wasp. It's alright.

PATRICIA. Ok, facts. There was an attempted rape. But you can't prove that. And then there was torture. You can prove that. Torture. You can't do that. But you did it.

TERRY. They'll throw the key away.

PATRICIA. Shut up, idiot! — I'm sorry. I appreciate your opinions, but they do not throw keys away. They have suspended sentence, plea bargaining, parole, probation. They have alot of things! Ok. We have isolated the problem. I don't know what to do. But I do know your lives are joined now. If he goes under, so do you. If he's kept well, so are you. And that's all I care about. You. Use the hammer, or don't use the hammer. At the moment you have a choice. But if he dies — and he could be dying right now — you have no more choice. And neither do I. So giving him alittle bread, to absorb the poison in his mouth, would be one very powerful witness of your humanity, and you need all you can get. One roll. Half a roll. For you.

MARJORIE. Do it.

PATRICIA. Thank you.

RAUL. That goes for me too. Could I have alittle sip of wine?

MARJORIE. No!

RAUL. Thank you just the same.

MARJORIE. If I hear that voice again, I'll tear him to pieces.

PATRICIA. Did you hear that?

RAUL. Pieces.

PATRICIA. Will you shut up please?

RAUL. Whatever you think's best, honey.

PATRICIA. I have bread for you.

RAUL. My hand's broke. Could you feed me, please?

TERRY. Don't put your hands in there!

PATRICIA. Why not? What can he do?

TERRY. He said he'd bite my hand off.

MARJORIE. I thought this had nothing to do with you.

TERRY. Kiss off.

PATRICIA. Okay, okay.

TERRY. Okay your ass.

PATRICIA. Marjorie? Do you think we could unlock it?

MARJORIE. No.

PATRICIA. We'll be careful.

MARJORIE. No.

PATRICIA. This bread's for you, not him.

MARJORIE. No.

PATRICIA. If and when I'm asked what I saw here, I truthfully don't know what I could say in your favor.

MARJORIE. That's good to know.

TERRY. Open it, goddamit! I'm not going to prison for you!

MARJORIE. Prison? You? Never. You do exactly what good little girls are supposed to. Nothing.

TERRY. You didn't get raped so don't tell me you can *do* something because you can't because I know because I got raped once and it was all my fault because I was dressed up like Tinkerbell in pink tights one size too small and half shot in the ass on beer and grass and my best girlfriend's father offered me a ride home and he took a shortcut through a cemetery and stopped behind this mausoleum . . . (*pause*) So what could I *do?* Tell? Ruin everybody? What for? You can't undo it. It's over. I lived. Besides, you know what they'd say. I asked for it. So I went to bed that night and made believe it was just a bad dream. But you, you didn't even get raped, and I'm not committing complicity for you. (*pause*)

MARJORIE. Open it.

PATRICIA. Thank you. (*pause*) What's the combination?

MARJORIE. Right 31, Left 40 . . .

PATRICIA. And the last number?

MARJORIE. I'll do it. (*MARJORIE undoes the lock. PATRICIA secretly butters a roll. MARJORIE wears the chain about her neck.*

PATRICIA. I'll feed you.

RAUL. Thank you very much.

PATRICIA. May I loosen the noose? He won't be able to swallow.

MARJORIE. Do it!

RAUL. Thank you very much.

PATRICIA. There.

RAUL. You're a very kind lady.

PATRICIA. Open up. Let me feed you.

RAUL. Thank you. You're very kind. Very kind lady. God bless you. Mmmmm. Good bread. Thank you for putting butter on it.

MARJORIE. You buttered it?

PATRICIA. Just alittle.

RAUL. Very kind. Beautiful person. Good bread. Best bread I ever ate. Where do you get bread like this? I'd like to pick up a loaf for my mother. Good crust. But not doughy inside. And so good with butter. You wouldn't happen to have alittle slice of meat with this bread, would you? Not good meat. Something that fell on the floor. Or a piece with alot of fat on it. Something nobody else would eat?

MARJORIE. Would you prefer ham and cheese or roastbeef?

RAUL. Roastbeef, thank you very much, please.

MARJORIE. Lettuce and tomato?

RAUL. Hold the lettuce.

MARJORIE. Mustard?

RAUL. You got mayo? (*MARJORIE prods him against the wall and gently touches his head with the hammer. Pause.*)

MARJORIE. Who the fuck you think you're playin wit, bitch. (*Pause. She spits in his face. Pause. She walks away. PATRICIA feeds RAUL. She lifts the edge of his blindfold.*)

PATRICIA. O my God. His face.

RAUL. What?

PATRICIA. Bubbled up. Blood's running out his nose. The ammonia burned his nose linings.

RAUL. You three are gonna get a snapshot, front and profile, down at the cop shop, jack.

PATRICIA. I'm going to the drugstore. For the atrophine.

MARJORIE. For my good, right?

PATRICIA. Why don't you look under the blindfold? Or is that why you covered it? You can't stand to see the damage you caused? I want that atrophine.

MARJORIE. I'll let Terry go.

TERRY. Where should I go?

MARJORIE. Drugstore at the mall.

TERRY. I'm broke.

PATRICIA. I blew my last few bucks on the cheesecake. Do you have any money?

MARJORIE. You want me to pay for the animal's medicine?

PATRICIA. Can I borrow it?

MARJORIE. I should've crushed his skull in the first two seconds, had it all cleaned up by time you got home, and never said a word. But I let myself talk, and in talk I squandered it. Talk, talk, talk, talk, talk. No phone calls.

TERRY. Alright.

MARJORIE. Say it.

TERRY. No phone calls.

MARJORIE. If you bring the police, I'll do it, Terry, and it'll be just like you did it. When I see 'em pull up, one hit, he's out, two, he's dead. Two seconds. That's all it takes. And I'll be watching every second. (*handing her the keys and money*) It should take seven minutes to get there, five in the store, seven to get back, even if you catch the light both ways. I give you one exta minute for the unaccountable. Seven, plus five, plus seven, plus one . . . Twenty minutes.

PATRICIA. Don't speed. You might get stopped. Get atrophine and something for burns.

TERRY. Astrophine . . .

PATRICIA. Atrophine. I'll write it down.

MARJORIE. One second after twenty and he's dead. And it'll be just like you did it. You. (*PATRICIA writes on a pad, hands it to TERRY. MARJORIE snatches it from TERRY's hands.*)

PATRICIA. Don't you trust anybody?

MARJORIE. Myself.

TERRY. Typical Leo.

PATRICIA. Just go.

RAUL. (*as TERRY opens the door*) Complicity. (*TERRY pauses in the door, exits. MARJORIE locks the door, marks the time, sits by the window. Long pause.*) Excuse me. Can I say something? (*Silence, which he takes as consent.*) I want to thank you very much for the bread. And for putting up that money for my medicine. I think that was very kind of you. Most people wouldn't go that far. But you want all-out and I'm all choked up and want to thank you from the bottom of my heart because it was generous and it was kind and it was nice. So nice of you. You wouldn't have an extra cigarette, would you? Or maybe one that was smoked halfway?

MARJORIE. Menthol filter alright?

RAUL. Thank you very much.

MARJORIE. Reach your hand out and I'll give it to you.

RAUL. No thank you. Bad for the lungs. (*Lights fade.*)

SCENE 2

Fifteen minutes later. MARJORIE sits at the window picking at her wasp stings. PATRICIA cleans the supper debris.

PATRICIA. Does it hurt bad? (*MARJORIE shakes her head no. Pause.*) Would you like a cup of tea? (*MARJORIE shakes her head no. Pause.*) Anything?

MARJORIE. Seventeen minutes.

PATRICIA. Did you pull the stinger out? (*MARJORIE

shakes her head no. Puase.) Would you like me to get
the tweezers?

MARJORIE. Please. (*Exit PATRICIA.*)

RAUL. Excuse me.

MARJORIE. Shut up.

RAUL. Can I say one thing?

MARJORIE. No.

RAUL. It's about stings.

MARJORIE. Want me to put your lights out?

RAUL. Forget it.

MARJORIE. (*pause*) What?

RAUL. Talkin to me?

MARJORIE. What do you think?

RAUL. What do I know?

MARJORIE. What about stings?

RAUL. Ain't no stinger in there.

MARJORIE. Says who?

RAUL. Wasp don't leave no stinger. A bee leaves a
stinger and croaks. But a wasp keeps on stingin.

MARJORIE. How do you know that?

RAUL. I know what I know. A wasp don't sing, a bird
don't sting. They're gonna call you Hammer. And one
night them hefty lesbies are gonna test your mojo, jump
you in your roachy piss-smellin six by ten, bust your
nose, make it flat, spit your teeth in a toilet bowl, and
when bull says get down in the bush, Hammer jumps in
the weeds smokin dry beever, cause you're like me, you
do what you gotta do to keep alive. And don't hollar
cause them hacks get a sudden case of deaf cause they
don't get involved in petty in-house business. So keep
your ass close to the wall or some cannibal puts a dull
screwdriver in your back and nobody hears nothin when
them showers are splashin and them radioes are blastin
them funky tunes and your blood washin down the

drain reminds you of once upon a time in a cozy little house, me and you, to have and to hold, forever.

PATRICIA. (*entering*) Here.

MARJORIE. There's no stinger.

PATRICIA. You pulled it out?

MARJORIE. Wasp doesn't leave a stinger.

RAUL. Best thing's to rub it with alcohol.

PATRICIA. We don't have rubbing alcohol.

RAUL. Got any hundred proof whisky or vodka?

PATRICIA. Hundred and fifty-one proof rum.

RAUL. Beautiful. Let me taste it first to make sure.

PATRICIA. Does it work?

MARJORIE. Very well, thank you.

RAUL. You're welcome. Anytime. I mean if we can't help each other out, what the hell are we on this earth for?

PATRICIA. Did Matilda come home?

MARJORIE. No.

PATRICIA. When'd you see her last?

MARJORIE. Don't remember.

PATRICIA. Was she in heat?

MARJORIE. Don't know.

PATRICIA. I think we should get her spayed. I can't stand it when she goes off looking for that red tomcat. Then I'm driving and I see a lump of bloody fur in the road—and it's just a possum, or squirrel. Would you mind if I got her spayed?

MARJORIE. Twenty minutes.

RAUL. Maybe she stopped for gas.

MARJORIE. She's a traitor.

RAUL. Maybe she ran into traffic. Her car needs a valve job. Ten to one she broke down.

PATRICIA. I'll make sure they put you away!

RAUL. Come in here motherfucker, I bite your throat! (*MARJORIE grabs RAUL's noose, raises the hammer.*)

RAUL. Hail Mary, full o' grace, smoke this loony bitch! (*PATRICIA grabs the hammer. They struggle. PATRICIA is hurt.*)

MARJORIE. I'm sorry.

PATRICIA. Don't touch me! (*TERRY's car pulls up.*)

RAUL. I'm fuckin saved! Blessed art thou among women! (*MARJORIE opens the door. Enter TERRY with a white drugstore bag.*)

MARJORIE. You're fuckin late, goddamn you!

TERRY. You killed him? For two minutes? (*discovering RAUL*) O.

PATRICIA. Where's the atrophine?

TERRY. You can't buy it over the counter.

PATRICIA. Why not?

TERRY. You need a doctor's signature.

MARJORIE. Did they ask questions?

TERRY. Why I needed it.

MARJORIE. And what'd you answer?

TERRY. Emergencies.

MARJORIE. Did they believe you?

TERRY. How should I know?

MARJORIE. What did you think?

TERRY. I don't know!

PATRICIA. Did they suggest a substitute antidote?

TERRY. You didn't say to do that.

PATRICIA. You should've figured that!

TERRY. I told 'em we live in a farmhouse and have alot of wasp trouble . . .

MARJORIE. Why'd you tell them where we live?

PATRICIA. Now what do we do without the antidote?

TERRY. They said see a doctor or go to the emergency room.

MARJORIE. Why were you so long?

TERRY. I ran into Sally in the parking lot. She's getting divorced.

MARJORIE. You talked with her?

TERRY. She wouldn't let go of my arm!

RAUL. Talkin in a parkin lot! You dippy bitch! She's gonna hammer me and you're talkin in a parkin fuckin lot!

PATRICIA. This isn't for burns! It's for cuts!

TERRY. That's all they had!

PATRICIA. I know they have it!

TERRY. Then go get it! I'm stick of being the goddamn gofer around here!

PATRICIA. A damn moron would've got a substitute antidote!

TERRY. Then send a damn moron next time! And if you can't find one, you'll do just fine!

PATRICIA. I'll apply this for whatever it's worth.

MARJORIE. Four dollars and fifty cents to be exact.

RAUL. Let me chip in. I pay my way.

PATRICIA. Shut up! May I take off the noose to apply the medicine?

MARJORIE. Why don't you just fuck him. Maybe that'll make him feel better.

TERRY. You both make me sick. (*PATRICIA seats RAUL with great difficulty.*)

RAUL. Thank you.

PATRICIA. Shut the fuck up! (*With great delicacy, PATRICIA removes the blindfold. TERRY gasps at the bloody sight.*)

RAUL. What was that? Terry? Why'd she do that? Am I ugly?

PATRICIA. No.

RAUL. Liar. I'm a fuckin monster.

PATRICIA. Open your eyes.

RAUL. I'm afraid.

PATRICIA. Open them.

RAUL. They open?

PATRICIA. Yes.

RAUL. I can't see. I can't fuckin see. Mother of God.

PATRICIA. I'm sorry.

RAUL. Go tell my babies sorry.

PATRICIA. Is there anything I can do?

RAUL. Give me a crown of thorns and finish me off!

PATRICIA. Why don't you have the honors! (*picking up hammer, handing it to MARJORIE*) Finish what you start!

RAUL. What the fuck's goin on here? Patti! You snake-face traitor! I pray for an angel, but what's god send me? A fuckin traitor! Fuck you and your bread! And fuck god! Fuck 'em! You're all gonna burn, baby! one, two, three, burn!

PATRICIA. How can I stop the pain?

RAUL. Give me back my eyes!

PATRICIA. What's your name?

RAUL. Mike.

PATRICIA. Mike what?

RAUL. Mentiras.

MARJORIE. How many women have you raped and murdered?

PATRICIA. You don't have to answer anymore.

MARJORIE. Tell them about the pothole crew.

RAUL. The *what?*

MARJORIE. When I rode by on my bike! Tell them why you came here!

RAUL. Use the phone. (*MARJORIE slaps his raw*

wounded face. He almost screams from his raw wounds but holds it in.)

MARJORIE. I'm sorry.

RAUL. She said, sure, come in and use the phone, and she was walkin around with her robe open, the red robe, with nothing much on underneath.

MARJORIE. Why are you looking at me like that?

PATRICIA. I'm not looking in any special way.

RAUL. And I'm usin the phone and she comes struttin pretty and ok, she turned me on, I admit it. I'm just a man. God made me that way. Something happens inside. Boom. And when I tried to go, she goes nuts, sprays me with this stuff, pulls the phone, starts yellin rape.

MARJORIE. Mother of God! You believe him!

RAUL. If that's a lie, let God off me on the fuckin spot! Now tell 'em about the hole, Marjorie! Tell 'em about the grave! My grave!

PATRICIA. What grave?

RAUL. O! I don't hear Marjorie talkin now! — Terry comes home and they decide to dig a grave in the garden and bury me!

PATRICIA. Is that true?

RAUL. Between the tomatoes and the flowers! With the possums and the dogs! A fuckin grave!

PATRICIA. That can't be true!

RAUL. Don't believe me. Let the grave talk!

PATRICIA. Is there a grave out there?

TERRY. Ask her.

PATRICIA. I'm asking you! The one who wanted to make up a story!

TERRY. I didn't dig it!

RAUL. See! See! Bury me alive, Patti! Alive! Whacko and Terry!

TERRY. Alls I did was watch him! Marjorie said she would drag him out, throw him in and cover it herself!

PATRICIA. Did you get enough justice today? Two eyes enough? Burn a man alive? Is that savage enough?

MARJORIE. Not as savage as a human roach forcing your legs apart!

RAUL. Awwwww, c'mon, c'mon, c'mon! What would I go do that for? Get some ass? I got poontang home.

MARJORIE. I thought your pregnant wife won't let you touch her?

RAUL. Don't talk about my sick wife, especially you, wit a sick father in the hospital.

MARJORIE. He stole our mail!

RAUL. I can't win wit this woman! First I'm a killer! Then I'm a raper. Now I'm a thief! What next?

MARJORIE. Don't you see what he's doing?

PATRICIA. Leave the man alone! Can't you see he's in pain?

RAUL. Don't say one bad thing about Marjorie. We're all human. We do things we don't mean, and I forgive her everything. All I wanted was a kind word, a little closeness, to forget my troubles; all she wanted was to forget about some guy in New York. Tony.

MARJORIE. Tony wrote to me and animal took one of the letters.

TERRY. He wrote you?

MARJORIE. I never answered.

TERRY. Why didn't you tell me?

MARJORIE. I didn't want to hurt you.

TERRY. Is that why he came here when he knew I was at work?

MARJORIE. Terry, please believe me.

TERRY. Is that why you changed from jeans to bathrobe when I brought him here.

MARJORIE. I must've been ready for bed.

TERRY. You're always ready for bed!

PATRICIA. You do dress loose, you know.

TERRY. Everytime I'd have a guy over, I'd have to shout in to see if you're decent.

PATRICIA. You parade around this house like it was a centerfold. A man enters the room and you go all statuesque. How you cross your leg at just the right moment— how you butterfly through a room—You're not happy until you're got every man in the room begging for it. And this one did. And now you want to fix him. One man pays for every letch and wolf whistle. You go through men like most women go through kleenex, and then you complain about the advances you provoke! The man is blind. Look at what you've done to yourself, to us, to him. Can't you look in blind eyes. Let's see what else you've done! (*She opens RAUL's jacket. Hanging from a leather thong is a curved hunting knife in a sheath. MARJORIE rushes to it, draws it out slowly. She lays the flat of it on RAUL's shoulder.*)

RAUL. I use it for work. (*pause*) I cut open boxes in a warehouse.

MARJORIE. Cut boxes, eh?

RAUL. Yeah.

MARJORIE. I thought you didn't have a job.

RAUL. O, I meant, you know, before I got employed.

MARJORIE. Cuts 'em good, eh?

RAUL. Yeah, pretty good.

MARJORIE. Sure, it's so sharp.

RAUL. Patti.

MARJORIE. And strong.

RAUL. Patti? You there?

MARJORIE. The kind of knife they use to gut a deer. Your move.

RAUL. Please.

MARJORIE. Smile. Nicer. Don't make your lips tight.

RAUL. Please!

MARJORIE. What's the matter?

RAUL. Patti! Terry! Make her stop!

MARJORIE. Know what you need? Acouple slashes here and here. Tell me you want it. Say it.

RAUL. O Mother of god, please!

MARJORIE. You're wrecking this for me. Say it.

RAUL. I want it.

MARJORIE. What?

RAUL. I want it.

MARJORIE. Want what?

RAUL. Please!

MARJORIE. Want what? Say it.

RAUL. The knife.

MARJORIE. Where do you like me to touch you? I forget.

RAUL. Nowhere.

MARJORIE. Remind me.

RAUL. Nowhere.

MARJORIE. Here?

RAUL. Nowhere.

MARJORIE. Or here?

RAUL. Nowhere.

MARJORIE. Ah, now I remember.

RAUL. Please! I beg you on my mother's milk!

MARJORIE. Down there! (*Putting the blade in RAUL's crotch and lifting him off the chair an eighth of an inch. Pause.*) Tell me you love it. Say it!

RAUL. I love it.

MARJORIE. Say it nice.

RAUL. I love it.

MARJORIE. Say it sweet.

RAUL. I love it . . .

MARJORIE. Sweeter!

RAUL. I love it.

MARJORIE. You say that beautiful. Again.

RAUL. I love it.

MARJORIE. Now tell me cut 'em off.

RAUL. I can't say that!

MARJORIE. This is your last chance.

RAUL. You can't make me say that!

MARJORIE. You say it and you say it nice and sweet and beautiful and you smile, you fucking bug, or I cut 'em off and stuff 'em in your mouth!

RAUL. Mother of god! I stole letters! watched the house! came here to fuck yous all!

MARJORIE. Who!

RAUL. You and Terry and Patti, like Paula Wyshneski and Linda Martinez, Debbie Parks and some I forget. They screamed. I begged 'em not to scream. I hate when they scream. (*MARJORIE runs a stiff hand across RAUL's throat. Thinking himself slashed, he writhes on the floor.*) Mother of god! (*realizing he's not slashed*) Thank you. (*pause*) Everytime I do it, it's in the papers, and I gets up in the morning and my wife and her mother they're talkin about it and I says, what happened? and they says, the raper got another girl last night, and they show me the paper and a picture of the dude somebody saw runnin away, but it don't look nothin like me. And my wife says, fix the back door, Raul, cause I don't want no raper comin in here, and I says, don't worry, he don't want you, and she bitches and I fix the door real good so the raper can't get in. (*pause*) Tell 'em lock me in a room. Not with locks. I know about locks. I can pick 'em. A room with nobody else. And maybe if I could have a little radio so's I could listen the ball game so it won't be so quiet because I hate the quiet because the dark, I don't care, but the quiet, please don't let it be quite.

MARJORIE. (*long pause*) I think you should go get . . . help.

PATRICIA. Ok.

MARJORIE. Keep Patricia company?

TERRY. Won't you be afraid?

MARJORIE. No.

PATRICIA. What do we say?

MARJORIE. Say a man is hurt.

PATRICIA. Ok.

MARJORIE. Say a man needs help.

PATRICIA. Ok.

RAUL. Marjorie?

MARJORIE. Yes?

RAUL. Can I say your name?

MARJORIE. Yes.

RAUL. One big favor?

MARJORIE. Yes.

RAUL. Don't make 'em put the siren on?

MARJORIE. Tell them no siren.

RAUL. And no red light?

MARJORIE. And no red light.

PATRICIA. Ok.

RAUL. Thank you very much. (*Exit PATRICIA and TERRY. Upon hearing the door close:*) You there?

MARJORIE. Yes.

RAUL. Thank you. Don't leave me alone?

MARJORIE. I'm right here.

RAUL. Thank you. They comin?

MARJORIE. Yes.

RAUL. Don't let 'em beat me?

MARJORIE. No.

RAUL. Thank you very much. You there?
MARJORIE. Yes.
RAUL. Marjorie?
MARJORIE. Yes?
RAUL. Can I wait in the fireplace?
MARJORIE. If you want.
RAUL. Thank you. (*getting to his knees*) Show me.
(*MARJORIE puts the knife down, directs him to the
mouth of the fireplace. He crouches inside, closes the
screen. Lights fade slowly.*) Thank you. Thank you very
much. (*He rocks slightly. Almost imperceptibly he sings
slowly, MARJORIE weeps.*)

Found a peanut
Found a peanut
Found a peanut just now
Just now I found a peanut
Found a peanut just now

Cracked it open
Cracked it open
Cracked it open just now . . .

(*Lights fade to darkness.*)

END

PROPERTY PLOT

FURNITURE

Wicker settee
Swivel arm chair
End table
Pedestal oak table
Three side chairs
Bench
Two area rugs (padded)
Metal headboard
Three throw pillows
Bicycle (wheel off)

PROPERTIES

Phone
Cassette player w/cord
Tea kettle
Hunting knife w/sheath
Scoop shovel
Insecticide
Hammer
Paint brush
Trowel
Metal ashtay
Ammonia bottle w/water
Bleach bottle w/water
Tool box
Ceiling paint roller
Paint box w/dressing
Wooden box matches
Hanging plants
Plant mister
Wine glasses

Wine bottle
Key hook
Pad of paper
Pencils
Iodine
Bite bandage
Bucket
Breakfast (dressing)
Plate w/coldcuts, bread
Bookshelf dressing
Planting dressing
Painting dressing
Bookshelf dressing
Mantle dressing

MARJORIE — Cigarettes, matches, lighter

TERRY — Bags of groceries, keys, purse
(Act II — Drugstore bag w/medicine)

PATRICIA — Cheesecake box, purse, keys, briefcase

RAUL — Knife harness, (padded), vest, belt, noose
   rigging

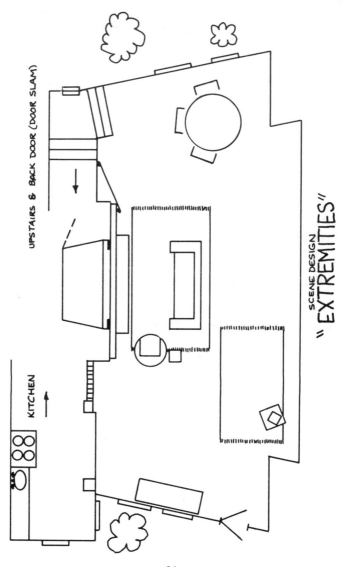

UPSTAIRS & BACK DOOR (DOOR SLAM)

KITCHEN

SCENE DESIGN
"EXTREMITIES"

THE MAKING OF EXTREMITIES

In May of 1978 I met a fifty-five year old woman. For convenience, let's call her Mary. Her face was cut, swollen and bruised. I didn't realize it then, but our conversation would alter the course of my life.

Mary was a rape victim. She told me she was raped the night before. Perhaps because I was a complete stranger, she told me about her bizarre ordeal. A nineteen year old man broke into her apartment with intent to rob. Thinking no one home, she startled him when she awoke. He raped her, beat her with a lamp and fled. Hours later, when she was able to pick herself up, she called the police and gave a description. She was given a humiliating pelvic exam at the hospital and taken to police headquarters to look at several suspects. Out of a line up of six, Mary made a positive identification of the rapist. He was arraigned and a court date set.

Months later the trial began. Mary was made to retell the rape before her peers, the public, the press. The rapist sat quietly in a three-piece suit, white shirt and tie. He looked like the son of a minister. When he was cross-examined he made amusing remarks. The jury laughed. There was evidence of rape but no evidence that *he* was the rapist. The case was dismissed. Mary left the courtroom. On the courthouse steps the rapist walked up behind Mary and said, "If you think that was bad, wait until next time."

Mary informed the police. They told her that they would keep regular patrols near her home, that she should call them on the slightest suspicion. But there are many hours in a minute when you're waiting for the rapist to return. The house plays such cruel little pranks. A board creaks in the middle of the night. The dripping faucet sounds like a man coming up the stairs on tiptoes. The wind. A cat. Mary slept with the light on. Next

to the phone. With a butcher knife. It was too much.
She quit her job, lost her pension, and bought a one-
way ticket to the opposite coast.

On her way to the airport, Mary stopped by to say
goodbye to me. If she hadn't, "Extremities" would not
exist. She thanked me for listening. We shook hands
and parted. As she walked through the door, something
possessed her to stop and turn and say: "There was a
moment during the rape when the animal stopped and
reached for one of my cigarettes on the night table . . .
He couldn't reach it . . . He put one foot on the floor . . .
At that moment I knew I could kick him and hurt him
. . . The moment waited for me . . . But I just lay there
. . . Paralyzed . . . Maybe it was that I was just brought
up not to hurt anybody . . . Maybe it was that I was too
afraid that if I didn't hurt him enough, he'd kill me . . .
I don't know . . . I did nothing . . . He lit a cigarette,
raped me again and then beat me with a lamp . . . I will
think about that moment for the rest of my life . . . I
will fantasize about what would have happened . . .
Now I can see myself hurting him . . . And hurting him
some more . . . It's hard for me to admit that I love to
hear his scream . . . I should have acted . . . I would've
got real justice . . . Not to act is to have to live with a
coward for the rest of your life . . . If I had five minutes
in a locked room with him now . . ."

Mary did not finish her sentence. "Extremities" was
written to fill in the blank she left. I had never seen such
anger in a woman except on stage in "Medea". Something screamed in me. I was sick and angry. Sick because
the woman's life was ruined. Angry because her peers let
a guilty man go. "Extremities" came out of me like an
overdue baby. I began writing that night at midnight. I
worked all night. I thought it was a two-character play,

but then Terry and Patricia walked in. I slept two hours at the end of Act One. By three that afternoon I had finished.

In the ensuing months, I began my research. When I heard of a rape trial, I would sit in the court all day. I talked to spectators, lawyers, sometimes defendants and plaintiffs. I learned that one out of three women in the U.S. are sexually assaulted by age eighteen. That of all rape cases that are able to pass strict rules of evidence, only two percent result in conviction, which means that its easier for a camel to pass through the eye of a needle than for a rapist to go to prison. That the average rapist rapes 29 times. That means 29 women. Most rapes go unreported due to embarrassment or fear. That juries are so fearful of sending an innocent man to prison many guilty men are set free. Now I began to fathom Mary's urge to rip the rapist to pieces.

I spoke with a lawyer who was defending a rapist. The conversation went something like this:

Q—How do you defend a rapist?

A—A man is only a rapist after he's convicted. At that time, defense is impossible.

Q—How do you defend a man who's been charged with rape?

A—Of course it's always different, but there's a certain recipe that helps—put as many women on the jury as possible.

Q—Women? Don't you mean men?

A—Women. Women attack other women. I don't know why. A man on the jury sees in the plaintiff his mother, sister, wife, lover, and that brings out the white knight in him. You can actually watch them strap on the armor and go to the rescue of a lady in distress. A woman, on the other hand, lives in constant fear of rape. I don't know if a man can really understand it. She tends to distance herself from the victim . . . She thinks, There, but for the grace of God, go I . . . Why didn't she lock her door? . . . What was she doing there? . . . Why was she dressed like that? . . . Women tend to blame other women for being raped because most women have accepted the male myth that some women like it, want it, crave it, in fact.

No producer dared to put "Extremities" on stage for two years. (Most producers are men.) Extremities went where it was welcome. The first production was in a community college by amateurs. The town council made a motion to ban the play—for which I now take time to thank them for the priceless advertisement. As a result, there was a playwright's dream every night—standing room only. The next production was in a hole in the wall in Philadelphia. The reviews ran the spectrum from loathing to worship (which has always been the trend). Audiences were less fickle. They loved it. Sometimes they threw things at Raul. One night several women ran on stage and tried to stop the attempted rape. Then there were two university productions, and then it went to one of the best regional theatres in America, Actors Theatre of Louisville, where it received worldwide attention. From there, the movie rights were sold and a New York production was planned. The New York critics ran the spectrum again, but the public voted at the box office in overwhelming favor. From there "Extremities" travelled around the world—Norway, Denmark, Sweden, Canada, Mexico, Australia, South Africa, France, Italy, Spain, Germany and Greece.

All because Mary had stopped to tell me her dark fantasy—to be alone in a locked room with the rapist. In giving her the five requested minutes—giving her, in fact, two hours—I had given thousands of women a fantasy that affects real behavior. Fantasy gives permission to reality. That is, what we allow ourselves to fantasize encroaches upon our everyday behavior. I know this because after every show, women, hundreds and hundreds of women, sought out the playwright, director, actors, to tell us of their rape experiences. There was a time in China's history, Confucius remembers, when historians left blanks in their books for what they didn't know or weren't sure of. That's the epitome of integrity. I wish playwrights could do the same. As I learned about this epidemic phenomenon, I changed the play. In one instance in Philadelphia, a woman in the audience screamed during the show. The actors stopped until she seemed to be alright and then continued. Later, the woman came to me and said, "I'm sorry I ruined your play. I was raped 20 years ago and forgot until tonight." That was the basis for Terry's monologue which I wrote that night and appended into the script.

As a man I have been reeducated about rape. The most dangerous teaching is the unconscious acceptance, the insidious little assumptions one makes while growing up. I have, through the play, freed myself of the two lethal myths. One, that women cause rape, and two, that rape is for sex. A woman can never cause rape. That is a male excuse for the desire to rape projected into the victim. Rape is done to degrade, humiliate and intimidate. It is a confusing issue because the tenderest act of man and woman is used to disguise the most brutal and sadistic. The extremities of the spectrum are brought together. Based on interviews of victims, the worst part of rape is not the physical. It is the fear, the threats, real or imagined, the degradation, the helplessness. "Extremities" has focused on the latter. Audiences often have to be reminded that no rape occurs in "Extremities". But audiences often *think* that a rape has occurred because of the mental cruelty of the first scene. We see Raul tossing Marjorie about like a tattered doll. We cannot know what is happening in her head. We can only surmise. We can only do that by giving something to the play, by investing emotion, by empathy. A play can only work when the audience is willing to project themselves into the protagonist in order to understand the character's thoughts and emotions. The audience must pay twice: once to get past the box office, and again to get beyond the footlights. When empathy comes easy, that is what we call a commercial play. "Extremities" is not a commercial play. There is no initial sales pitch to get empathy. But the audience gives it voluntarily. The fact that "Extremities" has gone so far is a tribute to audiences who think and feel for themselves.

"Extremities" contains the seeds of all the things that interest me as a writer — politics, ethics and morals, and psychology. A woman alone, a man enters, the play begins. From the very first, we see a contageon of violence pass from Raul, to Marjorie, to Terry, to Patricia. It grows in the language and in the action like a germ culture. The monster in all of us is just under the skin. Scratch the skin deep enough and it comes leaping out full-blown. In order to survive Raul, Marjorie has to become like Raul. To do that is to lose herself. The victim and victimizer, the cager and the caged, form each other. Thus, the psychological play leads to the moral play — How does one deal with evil without becoming evil oneself? Marjorie has a choice — to act or not to act. To turn Raul over to the police is a choice which would result in his release which would result in her death. Marjorie's self-preservation forces her to make another choice—to not release him, to bury him and assure herself he will never return. Standing so long on the verge of that choice, Marjorie equally fears what she will become after Raul is six foot under. There is no safe choice. On the one hand, her life is jeopardy. On the other, her sanity. She must act and act strongly, decisively. There is no help. Neither the authorities nor friends can lend a hand. Marjorie's helplessness leads to the politics of "Extremities", the idea of the violated social contract. Every individual and society make a deal: let's all surrender our state of nature, our animal impulses, in return for protection, in order to form an orderly society of rules by which we can all have freedom from each other. In "Extremities", Marjorie's actions are based upon the perception that society violates the social contract by not keeping up its end of offering protection. Sure, the police say, Call us when there's a problem and we'll come running, but what's that mean to a phi beta kappa prison graduate like Raul? Marjorie feels abandoned and therefore must defend herself against the most privileged citizen in our society - the recidivist criminal. And those who criticize me for Terry and Patricia's unfriendly reaction to Marjorie's dilemma had better turn their daggers to the two percent conviction rate first. Sadly enough, Marjorie's roommates' reaction is all-too-true. If "Extremities" could change anything, I would have it alter the perceptions of the people who sit in the jury box; I would have them hear testimony through the ear of the social contract. A play does not have to *say* anything. But it must *do* something. "Extremities" has changed people's perception of rape. The rest follows.

What some people have applauded or booed as 'comic relief' in "Extremities" is no such thing. I set out to re-create Mary's experience. I wanted to write a courtroom drama, not in court, but in a living room (where a woman is most likely to be raped, in her house). I wanted to create a psychic trial where all characters shift roles and become plaintiff, defendant, prosecutor, judge, jury, witness, etc. I wanted to show how the rapist can turn the jury around. In our society, we are all guilty of a prejudice. If some one makes us laugh, we think well of him. The rapists I have seen, and talked to, were cleverly rehearsed in their lawyer's offices, given a Sunday suit and a spitshine, and after an amusing remark, had spectators and jury saying, 'My, he's such a nice fellow — I don't think he could have done such a terrible thing" — That's the goal of every defense attorney, to let one positive trait through and let it begin that chain reaction that ends in a reasonable doubt. The result is a 98 percent chance of freedom for the rapist. To the horror of misunderstanding critics of "Extremities", audiences laugh. Alot. Where there is tension, there is need for release. Laughter is the most accessible form of release in the theatre. Raul has a certain devil-may-care variety of humor, but it's not for the sake of making mirth, but to turn people around, give doubt, divide, manipulate and finally destroy. He represents no social class or ethnic group. He only represents the men who know the law and how to beat the system. I have observed it countless times in courts and who doesn't like it, don't kill me. I'm only the messenger.

All theatre, in my opinion, is about change. We pay to see a character change. In change there is hope, and that is what I think an artist must do — not create false hope but dig as hard and deep as he can to find the best part of human beings. In the last scene of "Extremities" Marjorie's cycloptic drive to tear Raul apart results in a communication between victim and victimizer that goes beyond revenge. Marjorie does for Raul what all the social scientists, psychiatrists, police and prisons have failed to do — she gives him a conscience, and a soul. She makes him see himself from the other end of the knife. She makes him face himself. That is the beginning of change. Marjorie is exorcised of psychic torment, at the same time she gives Raul a soul. All theatre in my opinion, should be wish fulfillment tempered in reality. Women don't apprehend their rapists. Marjorie is the exception. But we can learn about the rule by examining the exception. So many rape victims have told me that "Extremities" has provided the catharsis that rape, police, lawyers, courts have not provided. That alone has made the entire experience worthwhile.

Down through the ages "Extremities" has been performed millions of times in the psyches of raped women who have mutely suffered the same brutalization and humiliation, and have, I am sure, in the privacy of their nightmares wielded hammers and broomsticks and brought about a justice that society denied them. I am only the one who wrote it down.

William Mastrosimone
Trenton, NJ 1984

Other Publications for Your Interest

SEA MARKS
(LITTLE THEATRE—DRAMA)

By GARDNER McKAY

1 woman, 1 man—Unit set

Winner of L.A. Drama Critics Circle Award "Best Play." This is the "funny, touching, bittersweet tale" (Sharbutt, A.P.) of a fisherman living on a remote island to the west of Ireland who has fallen in love with, in retrospect, a woman he's glimpsed only once. Unschooled in letter-writing, he tries his utmost to court by mail and, after a year-and-a-half, succeeds in arranging a rendezvous at which, to his surprise, she persuades him to live with her in Liverpool. Their love affair ends only when he is forced to return to the life he better understands. "A masterpiece." (The Tribune, Worcester, Mass.) "Utterly winning," (John Simon, New York Magazine.) "There's abundant humor, surprisingly honest humor, that grows between two impossible partners. The reaching out and the fearful withdrawal of two people who love each other but whose lives simply cannot be fused: a stubborn, decent, attractive and touching collision of temperments, honest in portraiture and direct in speech. High marks for SEA MARKS!" (Walter Kerr, New York Times.) "Fresh as a May morning. A lovely, tender and happily humorous love story." (Elliot Norton, Boston Herald American.) "It could easily last forever in actors' classrooms and audition studios." (Oliver, The New Yorker)

THE WOOLGATHERER
(LITTLE THEATRE—DRAMA)

By WILLIAM MASTROSIMONE

1 man, 1 woman—Interior

In a dreary Philadelphia apartment lives Rose, a shy and slightly creepy five-and-dime salesgirl. Into her life saunters Cliff, a hard-working, hard-drinking truck driver—who has picked up Rose and been invited back to her room. Rose is an innocent whose whole life centers around reveries and daydreams. He is rough and witty—but it's soon apparent— just as starved for love as she is. This little gem of a play was a recent success at New York's famed Circle Repertory starring Peter Weller and Patricia Wettig. Actors take note: *The Woolgatherer* has several excellent monologues. ". . . energy, compassion and theatrical sense are there."—N.Y. Times. ". . . another emotionally wrenching experience no theatre enthusiast should miss."—Rex Reed. "Mastrosimone writes consistently witty and sometimes lyrical dialogue."—New York Magazine. "(Mastrosimone) has a knack for composing wildly humorous lines at the same time that he is able to penetrate people's hearts and dreams."—Hollywood Reporter.

Other Publications for Your Interest

CAT'S PAW

(LITTLE THEATRE—DRAMA)

By WILLIAM MASTROSIMONE

2 men, 2 women—Interior

This is a gripping drama about terrorism; but it does not come at the subject in a way you'd expect. When we think of ''the terrorist'', we generally think of a wild-eyed religious or political fanatic. What if, posits the acclaimed author of *The Woolgatherer*, *Extremities*, *Shivaree* and *Nanawatai*, a terrorist came along who was brilliant, who was articulate and who was *right*? Victor is the head of a terrorist group which is responsible for a bomb attack against the White House in which 27 people have been killed. He has arranged to have a television news reporter led to his lair, there to tell the world why he has done what he has done. Victor's obsession is the destruction of the world's water supply, and with it the final destruction of the human race, by pollution. When the reporter asks him if he feels any guilt about the death of the 27 innocent people, he replies that hundreds of innocent people are dying every hour because of what mankind is doing to its water supply—and do the people responsible feel guilt for this? This cat-and-mouse game between the young woman reporter and Victor gets more and more tense, leading to a shocking and violent conclusion. A standing-room-only hit at Seattle Repertory Theatre and later at San Diego's Old Globe. ''An agonizingly suspenseful thriller.''—San Diego Tribune. ''A grabber.''—Seattle Times. ''Timely, thought-provoking and definitely worth seeing.''—San Diego Reader. ''Entertaining, informative, thoughtful and scary.''—The Weekly (Seattle).   (#5056)

SHIVAREE

(LITTLE THEATRE—COMIC DRAMA)

By WILLIAM MASTROSIMONE

2 men, 3 women— Combination interior

We are delighted to publish this lesser-known but wonderful play by the acclaimed author of *Extremities* and *The Woolgatherer*. The story concerns a young hemophiliac youth named Chandler who has been kept, of necessity, by his cab driver mother in a very sheltered sort of existence. Chandler is desperate for contact with the world. He is also highly intelligent; but is supremely naive about the ways of the world. He pays a neighbor to bring him a girl; but he can't go through with his plans to have sex with her. He just doesn't know what to do about his craving for love—until he meets Shivaree. She is another neighbor who supports herself by being an itinerant belly-dancer. She is a True Original, and before too long the delightful Shivaree and the innocent Chandler are in love, much to the consternation of Chandler's mother, who forbids Chandler to ever see Shivaree again, throwing Shivaree out of Chandler's room. Chandler, undaunted, climbs out the fire escape—his first venture outside his hermetic world—going after his love. Fans of Mr. Mastrosimone's other plays will recognize the true-ness of the characterizations and the poignancy and humor of typical Mastrosimone dialogue in this wonderful play.   (#21689)

Other Publications for Your Interest

A MAP OF THE WORLD
(ADVANCED GROUPS—DRAMA)
By DAVID HARE

7 men, 4 women, plus extras—2 Interiors

This new play by the author of *Plenty* "is an ambitious work which brings together in heated discussion a young left wing journalist and a right wing expatriate Indian novelist. The settings are a Bombay hotel where they are attending a world poverty conference and the British film studio where the Indian author's experiences are being turned into a film. Throughout the play, life and fiction overlap . . . One of the issues is the sexual jealousy that arises over the men's competition for the favours of a promiscuous American actress staying at the hotel. Also on the agenda: idealism vs. cynicism; the West's arrogance in its handling of Third World problems; the alleged evils of Zionism; and the journalist's fervent belief in the necessity for change."—London Sunday Express. "It is a pleasure to hear a stage echoing to such issues and such talk."—London Standard. "A rich and complex play built around a series of antitheses: the Third World and the West, fiction and reality, irony and commitment, reason and passion, the personal and the political. Yet for me what makes it the most mature and moving of Hare's works to date is its gut conviction that once we lose our Utopian dreams we have lost everything."—London Guardian. (#15620)

NANAWATAI
(ADVANCED GROUPS—DRAMA)
By WILLIAM MASTROSIMONE

10 men, 1 woman, plus chorus of female extras—Unit set

The intrepid Mr. Mastrosimone, heretofore the author of studies of character such as *The Woolgatherer*, *A Tantalizing*, *Shivaree* and *Extremities*, has here set his sights on an epic scale. Shortly after the Soviet Union invaded Afghanistan, Mr. Mastrosimone managed to get himself smuggled into that beleaguered country via Pakistan. There he spent several weeks with the Afghani rebels, observing their often futile attempts to resist the Russian blitzkrieg. All of the resistance he witnessed was not futile, though; he also observed the capture and execution of a Soviet tank crew. It was this incident which inspired *Nanawatai* (an Afghani word which means "sanctuary"). The story is told through the dual points of view of a Russian tank crew member and an Afghani rebel, as a chorus of village women impresses upon us the effect on the citizenry of all the bloodshed (not unlike, of course, in a Greek tragedy). "Hard-hitting and probing . . . alive with issues and conflicts of both a political and personal nature."—Hollywood Reporter. "It has the ritual power of Greek tragedy."—L.A. Times. (#15975)